WHAT EVERY HOME OWNER NEEDS TO KNOW ABOUT MOLD

AND WHAT TO DO ABOUT IT

VICKI LANKARGE

MCGRAW-HILL

NEW YORK   CHICAGO   SAN FRANCISCO   LISBON
LONDON   MADRID   MEXICO CITY   MILAN   NEW DELHI
SAN JUAN   SEOUL   SINGAPORE   SYDNEY   TORONTO

3 4 5 6 7 8 9 0   AGM/AGM   0 9 8 7 6 5 4 3

ISBN 0-07-141290-5

McGraw-Hill books are available at special discounts to use as premiums and sales promotions, or for use in corporate training programs. For more information, please write to the Director of Special Sales, Professional Publishing, McGraw-Hill, Two Penn Plaza, New York, NY 10121-2298. Or contact your local bookstore.

This book is printed on recycled, acid-free paper containing a minimum of 50% recycled de-inked paper.

For Ken, Matt, and Annelise

CONTENTS

PREFACE

I first heard the word "mycotoxins" in June 2001. I was scrambling to finish writing an article for insure.com about the insurance implications of a mysterious illness that had killed more than 500 thoroughbred foals in Kentucky. Scientists suspected that mold-based toxins in pasture grasses had caused the mares to spontaneously abort.

By the following day, my story was posted on the Web site and I was ready to write something new. That something turned out to be an article on a jury's $32 million verdict against Farmers Insurance Group for failing to cover the necessary repairs to a water leak, thereby allowing toxic mold to invade a Texas family's 22-room mansion. I didn't know it at the time, but toxic mold was about to become what lawyers are calling the "asbestos of the new millennium." I also was about to witness the unhinging of the Texas home insurance market, an event that has sparked consumer ramifications throughout the nation.

When news of the verdict broke, I was writing mainly about health and home insurance. I was naturally curious about a fungus that could not only damage your home but also weaken your immune system. And let's face it, this story had everything: A wealthy but ailing family forced to flee their contaminated home with only the clothes on their backs; a PR-savvy businesswoman who had the chutzpah and money to launch a full-scale holy war against her insurance company; and, later on, toxic mold lawsuits waged by activist-turned-celebrity Erin Brockovich and former Johnny Carson sidekick Ed McMahon, who says the fungus ruined his home, made him sick, and killed his beloved sheepdog, Muffin.

Who in the media could resist? It was like some crazy urban legend—except this one was real. Soon I was writing about mold at least once a week, sometimes more.

Today, virtually all home owners with access to newspapers, television, radio, or the Internet have heard at least something about "toxic" mold. Admittedly, much of what we hear is hysteria from one group trying to blame another for the problems caused by the fungus. But the mold crisis isn't really about blame. It's about loss.

Since 2000, insurance companies say they have suffered heavy financial losses due to mold and water-damage claims. Horrified, home buyers and sellers watch helplessly as their carefully negotiated deals crumble just hours prior to closing as previous mold and water-damage claims come back to haunt them. And then there are the men, women, and children who have no other option but to flee their homes or suffer the headaches, wheezing, and coughing associated with mold exposure.

I wrote this book out of respect for their losses and with the hope that it will help you protect your most valuable assets: your health and your home.

Vicki Lankarge
West Hartford, Connecticut

PART I

EVERYTHING YOU NEED TO KNOW ABOUT MOLD

CHAPTER
1

THE HOUSE OF PAIN

HOME IS WHERE THE BIOHAZARD IS

Melinda Ballard of Texas has a dubious distinction: She owns one of the most infamous homes in America. I only say "owns" because Ballard doesn't live in her Dripping Springs mansion anymore.

No one can.

Her 11,000-square-foot house and all of its contents—from a $65,000 silk Persian dining room rug to her family's photographs—are contaminated by a slimy black mold called *Stachybotrys* (pronounced "stack-e-BO-tris"). No one can enter this house without first donning a full decontamination suit and respirator.

This was supposed to be Ballard's dream house, a testament to her high-powered career as a New York City public relations executive and a haven for her and her husband, Ron Allison, and their young son, Reese. Instead, Ballard calls it her "house of pain," a place they fled in 1999 when Reese, then three years old, started spitting up blood, and Allison, suffering from memory loss, lost his job as an investment banker.

The mold began with several leaks in the drain system, leaks Ballard reported to Farmers Insurance Group. But after more than two years of haggling with her home insurer over repairs, Ballard says she had no other choice but to sue Farmers for fraud and bad faith because the company's actions resulted in mold overtaking her home. The mold infiltrated the home's air-conditioning unit, which then spread toxins throughout the house. At trial, experts testified that 10,000 square feet of mold (mostly *Stachybotrys*) had infested Ballard's home.

The trial garnered extensive publicity due to Ballard's media savvy and her take-no-prisoners approach. She took her crusade against Farmers to network television news programs, local and national radio stations, and the Internet. According to her lawyer, Houston attorney Fred Hagans, when Farmers began its campaign to delay and deny Ballard's mold claims, they picked the wrong person.

"Melinda wasn't going to take it lying down, or get frustrated, give up, and go away," says Hagans.

BALLARD V. FARMERS INSURANCE GROUP

The verdict heard 'round the insurance world was handed down in June 2001, when a jury awarded Ballard $32 million, including $12 million in punitive damages. Rarely had a jury awarded a home owner damages in a mold case against an insurance company, rather than against a builder or building owners.

This verdict was later gutted to just $4 million by the Austin 3rd Court of Appeals. In December 2002, the appeals court ruled that while there was sufficient evidence that Farmers had acted in bad faith in the Ballard case, there wasn't sufficient evidence that Farmers had committed fraud. (Ballard, who says her case isn't about money but about justice, is appealing the decision to the Texas Supreme Court.)

What is amazing about the original verdict is the jury made its landmark decision without ever hearing any direct medical testimony on how the mold had affected the family's health. This is because a Texas Supreme Court decision mandates a level of scientific proof that has not yet been reached in respect to the medical problems associated with *Stachybotrys*. But even without direct medical testimony, the jury sided with Ballard and Allison.

"This case wasn't about sympathy," says Hagans. "It wasn't about 'Poor brain-damaged Ronny.' It was about an insurer that failed to keep its promises."

The Ballard verdict has jury consultants scratching their heads. They believed the jury would be unsympathetic toward Melinda Ballard, a wealthy woman with a vibrant, sometimes aggressive, personality. Yet jury members identified with her, despite the fact that her dining room rug alone cost more than most people earn in a year.

"I think it was clear to them that I was fighting not just for my family, but for other home owners," says Ballard, who now maintains a database of more than 16,000 cases—dating back to 1985—where policyholders were forced to retain legal counsel to fight bad faith home insurance claims that began with water damage and resulted in mold infestations.

Jurors identified with Ballard because whether they lived in a 900-square-foot condominium in the city or a '50s-style three-bedroom ranch house in surburbia, they understood how awful it must be—both emotionally and financially—to lose your home. Consider this testimony from *Ballard* v. *Farmers Insurance Group:*

HAGANS: Would you describe for the jury how this has affected you and your family?

BALLARD: Well, needless to say, when you are stripped of everything that you own, it will turn your life, every facet of your daily routine, into complete and total upheaval. Imagine. Your home is your sanctuary. It is your retreat. It is where you go to kick back, lay back, do whatever it is that you want to do to relax. Imagine that suddenly taken away from you. Not just your home, but everything in it, considered a biohazard. And I go to the house every day to check to make sure I haven't been robbed, broken into, or vandalized. And I peer in my glass windows and I see everything in there, but I can't go in—without a

Hazmat suit and rubber gloves. I could never go in.

Certainly I can't use any of that stuff. It's all contaminated. All of my grandmother's items that I got . . . all of everything that I have collected in my life —at that point it was 41 years—I've lost. All of the memories. My child during his formulative years, this happened when he was three years old. Imagine a three-year-old kid who can't ride his tricycle because it's contaminated with *Stachybotrys*. . . .

Imagine what this would do to you. I am being sued by my neighbor for devaluing her property because my house sits as a toxic waste site, and she alleges that she can't even sell her home.

HAGANS: What words would you describe in terms of how it makes you feel?

BALLARD: Violated, deceived, raped, if you will . . . I used to be a size eight. I'm now a size two. . . . I don't know whether you consider that kind of rapid weight loss a benefit. I don't.

I've certainly not had the opportunity to sleep well at night over the last two years. It's just been a complete hell, an absolute hell. . . .

MOLD'S *PERFECT STORM* SCENARIO

Today, Ballard's mold problem is no longer hers alone. Every home owner throughout the United States is paying the price for rising mold claims and an extraordinary number of catastrophic losses, according to the Insurance Information Institute (III). Virtually unheard of prior to 2000, mold claims cost home insurers more than $1 billion in 2001. In Texas alone, Allstate Insurance Co., Farmers Insurance Group, and State Farm Insurance Co. lost $9.1 million during the first quarter of 2000 due to water-damage and mold-related claims. During the same time frame in 2001, that number exploded to $79.5 million. Fueling insurers' anxiety is the fact that they have collectively paid out more than $100 billion in catastrophe-related insured losses since 1989, including:

- $40 billion for the World Trade Center attacks (September 2001)

- $15.5 billion for Hurricane Andrew (August 1992)

- $12.5 billion for the Northridge, California, earthquake (January 1994)

- $4 billion for Hurricane Hugo (September 1989)

- $2.9 billion for Hurricane Georges (September 1998)

- $2.5 billion for Tropical Storm Allison (June 2001)

The rapid rise in mold claims combined with these catastrophic losses and a skittish stock market has created a kind of *Perfect Storm* scenario in which home insurance premiums nationwide have increased an average of 9 percent annually for the past few years.

And that figure is much higher for some—300 percent and more if you live in an area of the country with a high incidence of mold and you've made a water-damage claim or multiple smaller home insurance claims in the past few years. What's worse is that with your past claims history, you run a high risk of being dropped by your home insurer and you may find it difficult to obtain any alternate coverage.

Texas real estate broker Karen Wilson says it happens all too often in her state, where the home insurance market came unglued after several major insurers stopped selling new policies due to the rapid rise in mold- and water-related claims. But the problem is spreading nationwide, as insidiously as the black fungus that still creeps through Ballard's shuttered home.

"It's a crisis for both buyers and sellers," says Wilson. "There are properties with a past history of claims that are virtually uninsurable."

TEST YOUR KNOWLEDGE ABOUT MOLD

So what can you do to protect your home and your health?

Education is the key to mold prevention—or at least knowing how to address a mold infestation if it arises. Test your knowledge about mold by asking yourself the following:

- How can I tell if my home has mold?

- Which kinds of mold may cause health problems?

- What should I do if I find mold in my home?

- How can I find out if the home I'm buying has a history of mold or water-damage claims?

If you can't answer these questions, you need a crash course in mold. What you don't know about it could hurt you, your family, and the biggest investment you'll likely ever make: your home.

Follow me . . .

CHAPTER
2

THE FUNGUS
AMONG US

WHAT IS "TOXIC" MOLD?

There are over 10,000 species of mold. *Stachybotrys chartarum*, also known as *Stachybotrys atra*, is just one of many fungi that can produce "mycotoxins"—chemicals that can cause illness in people and animals.

Outdoors, mold helps decompose decaying organic material. It's found growing in soil, foods, and plant matter. Mold spreads by producing spores that are dispersed through the air. If the environmental conditions are right where the spores touch down, they form new colonies.

When molds are found indoors, however, they are less beneficial, to say the least. Indoors, mold can damage building materials, such as wallboard and ceiling tiles, and can cause health problems if it's allowed to flourish. If disturbed, mold spores may become "aerosolized," meaning that the spores may be dispersed through the air and then inhaled by a building's occupants. Without realizing it, you may have first heard or read something about toxic mold exposure more than a decade ago. While you may not be familiar with the words "toxic mold," you probably recognize the term "sick building syndrome," which describes health problems that appear to be linked to the time you spend in a particular building, although no specific illness or cause can be pinpointed.

Many of the symptoms associated with mold exposure are the same as sick building syndrome. Among these symptoms, according to the United States Environmental Protection Agency, are eye, nose, and throat irritation; coughing; difficulty in concentrating; and fatigue. Although the EPA cites inadequate ventilation and chemical contaminants as contributing to sick building syndrome, it also lists biological contaminants, such as bacteria, pollen, viruses, and molds, as suspected culprits.

But whether you call it sick building syndrome or mold exposure, the question remains: Why has the incidence of illness associated with mold risen so sharply in recent years?

Environmental experts say our modern building materials contain a higher degree of cellulose, an organic material that can foster rapid mold growth under the right conditions, including high temperatures and humidity.

These experts also say our modern buildings are more airtight, and inadequate ventilation encourages mold infestation. Just 50 years ago, building ventilation standards in the United States called for 15 cubic feet per minute (cfm) of outside airflow per building occupant, according to the EPA. But that standard was revised to just 5 cfm per occupant in 1973, as a result of the Arab oil embargo. So today, our energy-efficient homes burn less fuel to keep us warm, but they also retain more moisture.

HOW TO TELL IF YOUR HOME HAS MOLD

Every home has mold. It's just not always easy to tell where it is or if it's causing you or your family problems. The blackish growth on your shower stall is mold, but it's probably not toxic. Still, you should clean it up anyway. Even nontoxic mold can cause an increase in allergy symptoms. According to a 1994 Harvard University School of Public Health study of 10,000 homes in the United States and Canada, half had conditions of water damage and mold associated with a 50 to 100 percent increase in respiratory symptoms.

Stachybotrys is an uncommon mold. It's found in less than 1 percent of outside air samples and 6 percent of home samples, according to Dr. David C. Straus, a professor of Microbiology and Immunology at the Texas Tech University Health Science Center. It's unusual to find *Stachybotrys* in a home—unless your home has been flooded or otherwise suffered prolonged water damage.

What if you're not aware of any water damage, but you're still suspicious of musty odors and/or allergic symptoms?

Undetected leaks can cause hidden mold infestations deep within the walls of your home. So how can you truly tell if mold is growing in your home? Should you have your home tested?

Testing should *not* be your first course of action. These tests are expensive, and it's unlikely that your home insurer will pay for them. You can investigate on your own. It's more important to get rid of the mold and fix any underlying water problems than to spend a lot of money trying to find out exactly which of the 10,000 species lives under your kitchen sink. If you smell an earthy or musty odor, your home may indeed have mold. Your suspicions should be strengthened if the allergy symptoms of your family members or visitors worsen when in your home but disappear when they leave it. Additionally, if you see any evidence of water damage, such as staining of the wallboard underneath a window after it rains, then your home probably has mold. Con-

---

Note: Mold comes in many colors, including black, green, gray, and brown. Sometimes it may appear to have splotches of pink or purple. When it's actively growing, Stachybotrys *looks greenish black and shiny and may appear white around the edges.*

tributing factors to mold infestations are moderate temperatures and high humidity. The optimal temperature for mold growth is between 68 and 86 degrees Fahrenheit, which is why homes in the South and West are particularly susceptible.

Where should you look for mold?

Anywhere there is cellulose, mold's favorite food source, which is also vulnerable to leaking water, condensation, or high humidity. Typical places include:

- Basements or cellars that have been flooded

- Underneath kitchen and bathroom sinks

- Underneath or behind refrigerators

- Behind walls that also house plumbing

- Stacks of damp or wet newspapers or cardboard boxes

- Around air-conditioning units

- Wallboard around windows that leak

- Under carpeting that may have become wet

According to the Insurance Information Institute, there are several warning signs of mold that home owners should be on the lookout for, including:

- Sunken areas in baseboards or trim. These indentations appear when mold has consumed the wood behind the paint. The paint itself is often cracked or peeling.

- Separation of the baseboard from the wall or floor.

- Whitish mats under carpet, linoleum, in cabinets, or even behind furniture.

- "Fruiting bodies," or mushroomlike growths on rotten wood on the underside of flooring or a cabinet. Fruiting bodies are flat, up to a half-inch thick, and a pale olive, gray, brown, or black.

- Staining, swelling, or crumbling of plaster or Sheetrock.

- Discoloration (blackish staining) around air-conditioning vents.

- Vinelike branches from the soil to the foundation, framing, or underside of flooring. Vines are typically white, brown, or black and are called *rhizomorphs*. The fungus forms these vines that connect the soil to the wood.

RHIZOMORPHS

Even if the mold in your house doesn't make you sick, once these vines become established, "dry rot" may set in and severely damage your home. Dry rot is caused by these vines creeping through your home's timbers—

even through masonry—and transporting moisture to parts of your house that are not yet infested, hence the name "dry" rot. Cracks in the wood fiber then act like straws, siphoning up moisture and spreading more decay. Once the infested wood dries, it shrinks and breaks up into small, irregular chunks, weakening the timber's integrity.

Known as *Poria incrassata,* this water-conducting fungus may be mistakenly identified as a termite infestation because wood damaged by termites can resemble wood damaged by fungus. Adding to the confusion is the fact that both infestations occur under similar circumstances—where there's moisture and wood in contact with soil. Prime habitats are dirt-filled cellars, damp crawl spaces, porches, and wooden steps.

A savvy building inspector or exterminator, however, will be able to determine if the damage is primarily caused by termites because he or she will find further evidence of the insects, including their "mud tubes," or tunnels the termites use to travel from their nests to their water source.

WHY MOLD, WHY NOW?

Science tells us that mold has long been with us. A German microbiologist has even suggested that toxic mold spores—not some "Curse of the Mummies"—actually sickened ancient Egyptian tomb raiders and, later on, archaeologists seeking the secrets of the Pyramids. Gotthard Kramer has identified several kinds of potentially toxic mold spores on each of 40 mummies. He's concluded that it's possible when the tombs were first unsealed, a rush of fresh air stirred the still-living mold spores into the air, where they were inhaled by the tombs' trespassers. Because of these potentially harmful spores, it's now standard procedure for archaeologists working with mummies to wear full decontamination suits.

Note: Mold was a problem even back in biblical times. According to Leviticus, 14:39–47, "On the seventh day the priest shall return to inspect the house. If the mildew has spread on the walls, he is to order that the contaminated stones be torn out and thrown into an unclean place outside the town. If the mildew reappears in the house after the stones have been torn out and the house is scraped and plastered, it is a destructive mildew and the house is unclean. It must be torn down—its stones, timbers, and all the plaster—and taken out of town."

But if mold has always been with us, then why is it only in the last few years that we have started hearing about its potential to harm our dwellings and us?

According to Melinda Ballard, there wasn't much literature available in 1999 about the harmful effects of mold when she went looking for answers for her family. Ballard compares the growing public awareness about mold to the overall increased knowledge about many microorganisms, including *Escherichia coli*. Although this bacterium normally lives in our intestines without causing any problems, it can sicken and even kill if an individual unwittingly ingests a particularly virulent strain. After all, who among us now hasn't heard about the dangers of *E. coli* and the benefits of hand-washing after handling raw meat?

There is much less scientific study about the dangers of *Stachybotrys,* particularly when inhaled, according to Dr. Straus of Texas Tech. This is partly because *E. coli* can be cultured from an infected human being and studied, whereas *Stachybotrys* cannot. Although the mycotoxins produced by *Stachybotrys* can sicken people by wreaking havoc with their immune response, the toxic mold does not "grow" inside them once they've ingested or been exposed to it. In addition, the mycotoxins are hard to study because they're so small.

Dr. Straus says the *Trichothecene* mycotoxins produced by *Stachybotrys* are only 20 to 30 times larger than an oxygen molecule and can probably penetrate the most scientifically advanced high-efficiency particle-arresting (HEPA) respirators, even though this hasn't

Just how harmful are Trichothecene *myco-toxins? Although officially unconfirmed, there is a body of scientific evidence that supports the contention that* Tricothecene *mycotoxins were used as biological warfare agents in Southeast Asia and Afghanistan during the 1970s and 1980s by the former Soviet Union and its allies, according to Robert W. Wannemacher, Jr. and Dr. Stanley L. Wiener in their chapter on* Tricothecene *mycotoxins in the* Textbook of Military Medicine, *published by the Office of the Surgeon General. According to the authors, survivors of these "yellow rain" attacks reported skin rashes, burning in their noses and throats, blurred vision, vomiting, and diarrhea, among other symptoms.*

been conclusively proven. HEPA filters were developed by the Atomic Energy Commission during World War II to remove radioactive dust from nuclear plant exhaust. But lack of overwhelming scientific evidence won't prevent you from possibly falling severely ill after exposure to toxic mold. Just ask Dr. Straus. Within 30 minutes of entering Melinda Ballard's home in 1999 to conduct his investigation, he felt dizzy and vomited. To this day the professor has not regained a partial hearing loss in one ear, a problem he says he can date to the day he stepped inside Ballard's home without a "moonsuit."

"At the time, we had no idea how bad it was inside that house," he says. The point is moot now, anyway. Dr. Straus says he will never again step inside a mold-infested building—with or without a respirator. He has suffered toxic mold poisioning twice in his career—once before the Ballard exposure—and he does not want to jeopardize his health again.

CHECKLIST: WARNING SIGNS OF MOLD

Check all that apply to your home.

☐ My home (or an area in my home) has an earthy or musty odor.

☐ There is staining of the wallboard or wallpaper near a window, on a wall that houses plumbing, on an air-conditioning vent, or in some other part of the house that comes in frequent and/or prolonged contact with water or moisture.

☐ There are identations in my home's base-boards or trim.

☐ There are whitish mats under the carpet, linoleum, in cabinets, or behind furniture.

☐ There are "fruiting bodies" (mushroomlike growths) on rotten wood on the underside of flooring or a cabinet.

☐ There is swelling or crumbling of plaster or Sheetrock.

☐ There are rhizomorphs (vinelike branches) growing from the soil to my home's foundation, framing, or the underside of flooring.

MOLD IS NOTHING TO SNEEZE AT

SYMPTOMS OF MOLD EXPOSURE

The health problems linked to *Stachybotrys* first came to light in Russia and Eastern Europe in the early 20th century when horses that had been eating moldy hay fell ill. Those that had eaten more of the mold-infested straw were more likely to die from weakened immune systems, infection, and bleeding. The first recorded human victims were agricultural workers who handled this moldy hay and suffered rashes and itching, as well as coughing, headaches, and fatigue.

Mold is ubiquitous. Everyone comes in contact with many kinds of mold each day, usually without any harmful side effects. However, exposure to mold can provoke allergic symptoms in some people similar to hay fever, including:

- Nasal and sinus congestion

- Coughing

- Wheezing or difficulty breathing

- Skin and/or eye irritation

- Upper respiratory infections, including sinus

According to the Centers for Disease Control and Prevention (CDC), less common and less well-documented are cases where mold exposure may cause unusual health conditions, such as memory loss or lung hemorrhage. "These case reports are rare and a causal link between the presence of the toxic mold and these conditions has not been proven," the CDC concludes.

Although there are more common indoor molds, such as *Aspergillus, Cladosporium,* and *Penicillium, Stachybotrys* has received the lion's share of intense media attention—some say hysteria—because the mycotoxins it is capable of producing are quite powerful. Yet molds that have the ability to produce toxins don't always do so.

Detecting *Stachybotrys* is often difficult because the wet conditions these molds favor, such as those caused by a plumbing or roof leak, may be hidden from view and can go undetected for quite some time. The problem of identification is also compounded by the fact that several kinds of mold or bacteria may be found in conjunction with *Stachybotrys*. Also, there is currently no test that can conclusively demonstrate that you have been exposed to *Stachybotrys* or its mycotoxins. It's usually a case of putting two and two together—health problems in combination with evidence of a home's mold infestation.

> *Note:* There are no established standards
> for acceptable levels of indoor mold.

WHO IS MOST VULNERABLE?

Diagnosis is tricky because no one knows exactly how much *Stachybotrys* makes you sick. This is because people vary in their susceptibility to mold. You're most likely to be affected by *Stachybotrys* if:

- You have a respiratory disorder, such as asthma or chronic obstructive pulmonary disease.

- You have an immune system already weakened by cancer or HIV.

- You're either very old or very young.

The exposure of babies and children to *Stachybotrys* is of particular concern. Since 1994 in Cleveland, Ohio, there have been 45 cases of pulmonary hemorrhage (bleeding in the lungs) in babies under six months old, the majority of whom lived in water-damaged homes contaminated with high levels of *Stachybotrys*. Sixteen of the infants died.

According to Cleveland pediatric pulmonary specialist Dr. Dorr Dearborn, while the link between *Stachybotrys* and lung hemorrhage in infants has not been conclusively proven, it appears the powerful mycotox-

Note: On April 6, 1998, the American Academy of Pediatrics Committee on Environmental Health released a statement concerning toxic effects of indoor molds and pulmonary hemorrhage in infants. They recommend that until more information is available on this condition, infants less than a year old should not be exposed to any moldy or water-damaged environments.

ins that produced the mold may be quite harmful to the rapidly developing lungs of young babies. Dr. Dearborn says that when babies breathe in the mycotoxins, the blood vessels in their lungs may become fragile. The weakened vessels may become further stressed by illness or other environmental contaminants, such as cigarette smoke, and start to bleed.

This condition is rare. However, Dr. Dearborn advises that if your child is having nosebleeds without any signs of injury, you should seek medical attention right away. If your child has a chronic cough, chest congestion, and is anemic, you should ask your pediatrician to consider the possibility of pulmonary hemorrhage among all the other more common diagnostic possibilities. For more information on pulmonary hemorrhage in infants, visit the Pulmonary Hemorrhage and Hemosiderosis in Infants Web site at www.gcrc.meds.cwru.edu/stachy/default.htm.

Note: *Today, much attention is focused on the "bad" kinds of mold, such as* Stachybotrys. *But did you know that one of medicine's best-known wonder drugs is synthesized from mold? In the late 1920s, Dr. Alexander Fleming of St. Mary's Hospital in London discovered that a chemical he had isolated from the mold,* Penicillium notatum, *had prevented the growth of a nearby colony of germs in the same petri dish. Several years later, Howard Florey, Ernst Chain, and Norman Heatley expanded on Fleming's work at Oxford University by growing, extracting, and purifying enough penicillin to prove its value as an antibiotic. Visit www.herb.lsa.umich.edu, home of the University of Michigan Fungus Collection, for more information.*

MOLD DOESN'T DISCRIMINATE

It isn't just infants and the elderly who may be sickened by mold. In 2001, environmental activist Erin Brockovich testified before the California legislature that she, her husband, and their three children were battling mold-related illnesses due to mold that had contaminated their home. Appearing with Brockovich were California home owners Steve and Karen Porath, who had their mold-infested home burned down after they came down with chronic breathing problems and their son, then two years old, began to vomit, sometimes vomiting as many as 70 times a day.

Mold doesn't discriminate by your age, race, income, or occupation. It can grow in a 100-unit apartment complex in Brooklyn, New York or a 22-room mansion in Beverly Hills, California. It only needs four things to survive: food, moderate temperatures, oxygen, and water.

CHECKLIST: ALLERGIC SYMPTOMS THAT MAY BE RELATED TO MOLD

Check all that apply to you or your family. Contact your family physician if you suspect an allergy to mold that is not currently being treated.

- ☐ Nasal and sinus congestion

- ☐ Coughing

- ☐ Wheezing or difficulty breathing

☐ Skin and/or eye irritation

☐ Upper respiratory infections, including sinus

☐ Difficulty concentrating, memory loss

☐ Nosebleeds, cough that produces blood

Do the symptoms ease or stop altogether when you (or your family member) are away from home?

☐ Yes   ☐ No

Can you rule out other possible causes of these symptoms, such as allergy to pets or new carpeting, chemical sensitivity, or seasonal allergies?

☐ Yes   ☐ No

CHAPTER 4

WHAT'S MOISTURE
GOT TO DO WITH IT?

WATER IS MOLD'S BEST FRIEND

Mold needs water to grow. It thrives wherever there is a food source that is exposed to moisture. Homes that are particularly vulnerable to mold are those that have been flooded. Within 24 to 48 hours after floodwaters have receded, mold can begin growing on water-soaked materials, such as walls, floors, carpeting, books, clothes, and furnishings.

But water damage doesn't have to be so dramatic in order for mold to flourish. Anywhere water enters your home, you have the potential for extensive damage. Wood that is constantly wetted by a lawn sprinkler or walls that are frequently bathed in unvented shower steam can harbor an infestation. You should suspect mold if you have any places in your home that are subject to constant moisture, condensation, or steam, as well as periodic flooding or leaking.

Additionally, you should thoroughly inspect your home if you observe *any* of the signs of water damage listed in Chapter 2.

TIPS TO PREVENT MOISTURE AND MOLD

Extensive mold remediation can cost thousands of dollars, so the best way to avoid the hefty bills resulting from an infestation is to stop one before it starts. One way to inhibit the potential for mold growth is to keep indoor humidity at less than 50 percent. Check your home's humidity by using an inexpensive *hygrometer*, an instrument that measures the water vapor content of the air. You can find hygrometers in some home improvement stores and on the Internet.

According to the Insurance Information Institute, you can reduce indoor humidity by:

- Venting bathrooms, dryers, and other moisture-generating sources to the outside

- Using air conditioners and dehumidifiers

- Increasing ventilation

- Using exhaust fans whenever cooking, dish washing, and cleaning

You should also prevent the potential for condensation on cold surfaces by adding insulation to windows, piping, exterior walls, roof, or floors. Additionally, don't install carpeting where there is a perpetual moisture problem, such as bathrooms, or on concrete floors with leaks or frequent condensation.

The Insurance Information Institute also advises that you should:

- Fix plumbing leaks immediately.

- Keep your home's exterior painted.

- Keep flower beds away from exterior walls so the soil doesn't touch your home's siding.

- Don't wet walls with lawn sprinklers for a long period of time. This can allow the fungus to form rhizomorphs, so even when the sprinklers are off, the decay continues.

- Make sure the grade of your lawn slopes away from your home and there is adequate drainage. You don't want water from sprinklers or heavy rain to pool around your home.

- Don't pile wood or other debris in crawl spaces or against the sides of the house.

- Further inspect your home if you see evidence of bugs, such as roaches or termites.

- Where you have bugs, you usually have water.

- Further inspect your home if you see evidence of the fungus. Remember: The fungi can be tricky. The place where you see the fungus may not be the point of origin.

THE TOP THREE SOURCES OF WATER DAMAGE AND TIPS TO AVOID THEM

While the number of water-related home insurance claims varies from year to year, insurers say the amount of money they pay out for water-related damages has skyrocketed over the past few years. "Water represents a disproportionate share of the claims payments made on home owners' insurance policies," says Candysse Miller, executive director of the Insurance Information Network of California. For some insurers, says Miller, annual water losses account for as much as 40 percent of all home insurance claims payments. In addition to hiking home insurance premiums and restricting coverage, it's little wonder that insurers are now also trying to educate home owners about common sources of water damage.

According to data compiled by Allstate Insurance Company and the Insurance Council of Texas, the three most common sources of water damage in homes are *washing machine hoses, shower tile grout,* and *water heaters.* But the good news is that you can prevent these causes of water damage by using common sense and a regular home maintenance schedule.

While you should strive to check these three sources once a month, what's important is to start checking right away and to develop a regular routine. If you make a monthly mortgage payment or pay a monthly home insurance premium, this could serve as a meaningful reminder for you to inspect:

WASHING MACHINE HOSES

Washing machine hoses carry pressurized water even when your machine is not in use. If one bursts, it can fill an entire floor in your home with several inches of water. That's why you should always turn the water shut-off valve to your washing machine to Off after each use. According to the Insurance Council of Texas, it's best to check hoses for leaks or signs of deterioration once a month and replace them before they fail. (Hoses typically last between two and five years, depending on their initial quality. Hoses with external steel braided wire are a little more expensive than rubber hoses—$10 as opposed to $5—but have a lower failure rate. Contractor Greg Long, whose Texas-based TPV Group has become one of the leaders in the Texas mold remediation market, urges consumers to be on the safe side and replace their washing machine hoses at least every other year.)

Tips: When you replace the hose, remember to first shut off the water supply to the washer. Make sure the new hose is free of kinks and tight bends when it is installed. Keep at least four inches between the water connection and the back of the washing machine.

SHOWER TILE GROUT

Water that seeps through cracks in grout and caulk, especially in your shower, can rot the wooden structure of your home. If the bathroom is located on a second floor, a leak that is not quickly repaired could cause serious structural damage.

Tips: Inspect your shower once a month for any cracks or missing grout in between the tiles. If grout is missing, repair it right away by either regrouting it yourself or hiring a professional. The caulk arund the tub and sink needs to be checked and replaced periodically as well. And don't forget to check the shower pan for leaks! Leaky shower pans need to be repaired or replaced immediately.

How to apply grout:

- Remove old grout with grout saw. This will remove soap that has settled between the tiles.

- Clean the surface of the tiles.

- Mix grout according to the instructions on the package.

- Apply grout to the surface with a grout float (like icing a cake). Spread the grout into the seams between the tiles in a diagonal direction.

- Let the grout sit, according to the directions, typically 10 minutes.

- Wipe down the surface with a barely damp sponge. This will remove any excess grout on the tiles.

- Let dry for another 10 minutes or until you see a white haze (from dry grout on the tiles). Buff out the haze with a dry cloth.

WATER HEATERS

Do you know how much water is in your water heater? Some water heaters may hold up to 80 gallons of water, and if ruptured, they can flood an entire house. Partially drain your home's water heater every six months to keep sediment from building up on the bottom. This sediment can cause erosion and rusting of the tank lining. By periodically draining the tank, you may prolong the life of the appliance. Also, check for leaks in the draincock, safety valve, and plumbing connections.

Tips: Use **EXTREME CAUTION** *when draining the tank because the water inside is very hot. Additionally, if your home pumps well water instead of city water and a softening system is required, use potassium instead of a salt-softening system. Salt is more corrosive than potassium and can corrode copper pipes faster. This corrosion can cause pinhole leaks.*

How to partially drain a water heater:

- Turn off the electricity or the gas supply, depending on the type of heater you have.

- Attach a hose to the drain valve at the bottom of the tank and lead it to a nearby floor drain or into a bucket.

- Let the water drain until it becomes clear, typically a gallon or more.

- Close the drain valve and open the cold water supply to refill the tank.

- When this is done, restore the power or gas to the heater.

CHECK YOUR HOME'S WATER PRESSURE

You know what happens when you roll a capped tube of toothpaste too tightly. Well, the same thing happens to highly pressurized water that cannot escape from an open spigot or running appliance. The water has to go somewhere, and all too often it bursts through a pipe or appliance connection.

Tip: Routinely check your home's water pressure. The ideal pressure is somewhere in the range of 60 to 80 pounds per square inch range. Anything above that range has the potential to wear out the washers in your faucets and/or cause a leak. You can check your water pressure by purchasing a water pressure gauge at a local home improvement center. To determine water pressure, attach the gauge to an outdoor faucet and turn water on full to determine the pressure. Make adjustments as necessary or contact a plumber to adjust it for you.

CHECK YOUR HOME'S AIR CONDITIONERS

The cooling coils and condensation pans in stand-alone air conditioners are prime candidates for mold contamination. Check these for signs of mold and mildew. While you may feel up to cleaning a small patch of mold growing on your air conditioner's coils yourself, more extensive remediation may call for a professional.

Also, make sure wall units are sloped to the outside of the house. Air-conditioning units that are level or slope toward the house may allow water to seep into your house and result in a mold infestation.

CHECKLIST: ROUTINE MAINTE-NANCE TO HELP PREVENT MOLD

Inspect your home for water damage or mold regularly—once a month if possible. Try using your mortgage due date as a reminder to perform this check.

Check all that apply to your situation.

☐ My home's exterior is painted; there is no unfinished wood exposed to the elements. The siding does not come in contact with any flower beds or spray from a lawn sprinkler.

☐ There is no wood or other debris in crawl spaces or stacked against the sides of the house.

☐ My home shows no signs of a plumbing leak.

☐ My washing machine hose is connected properly and shows no sign of excessive wear and tear.

☐ The caulk around the tub and sink is in good condition, with no cracks or missing caulk. The same goes for the grout in between the shower tiles.

☐ There are no leaks in the draincock, safety valve, and plumbing connections of my water heater. I have partially drained the tank within the past six months.

☐ My home's water pressure is between 60 to 80 pounds per square inch.

PART II

You've Got Mold. Now What?

WHAT TO DO WHEN YOU SPOT MOLD

Okay, so one day you're on your hands and knees, thoroughly scrubbing your toilet (or tub, or shower), and there it is—a black patch of mold growing on the porcelain that is slick from condensation or shower steam. There's absolutely no need to panic. If caught soon enough, a small patch of mold can be cleaned up before extensive damage occurs.

TIPS FOR CLEANING A SMALL INFESTATION

Here are some tips if you plan on trying to clean up the mold yourself:

- Make sure you're free of allergy symptoms and/or asthma.

- Wear a mask and rubber gloves during cleaning.

- Using water and detergent, scrub mold off nonporous surfaces and dry completely.

- Absorbent materials may have to be discarded if they are moldy. It is likely that hidden mold lurks beneath the surface and will grow back and fill in the crevices

- Dispose of any sponges or rags used to clean the mold.

If the mold quickly returns or spreads, it may indicate an underlying problem such as a leak. Any underlying water problems must be fixed to successfully eliminate further problems. If the contamination is extensive—particularly if heating, ventilating, or air conditioning systems are involved—you will have to seek professional help from a mold abatement specialist. Don't paint over moldy surfaces. The paint will peel and won't kill the mold. Clean the infestation and dry all surfaces completely before any repairs.

Note: *The Environmental Protection Agency does not advocate using bleach (or any cleaners other than detergent) to clean small mold infestations. This is because many household cleaners contain toxic substances (called dioxins) that form in the making of organic chemicals that contain chloride.*

GUIDELINES ON THE FIVE LEVELS OF MOLD REMEDIATION

There are five different levels of mold abatement, and the size of the mold infestation determines the type of remediation, according to the New York City Department of Health. The goal of any remediation is to remove or clean contaminated materials in a way that prevents the fungi and dust contaminated with fungi from leaving the work area and contaminating someplace else, while protecting the health of the mold abatement workers.

The department recommends that the simplest and quickest remediation that properly and safely removes mold from your home should be used. Additionally, you must identify and fix the underlying cause of water accumulation or the mold growth will return. You must repair all water-damaged areas and prevent any further contamination through routine home inspections and home maintenance.

Mold remediators say that structurally sound items made of concrete, glass, hard plastic, metal, and some wood can be cleaned using a detergent solution and reused. Porous materials such as ceiling tiles and insulation, and wallboards with more than a small area of contamination (10 square feet) should be removed and discarded. Although some fabrics that can be cleaned may be reused, it's better just to throw them away. Routine inspections should always be performed to confirm whether the remediation process has been effective.

Note: The remediation and repair of your home can cost thousands of dollars, so it's important to be choosy when you're hiring a mold remediation specialist. Seek out other home owners who have experience in mold remediation and selecting contractors. Additionally, contact your local Better Business Bureau to learn whether any of the contractors you are considering have any complaints filed against them.

The average home owner shouldn't attempt to clean a mold infestation higher than a Level I without the help of a health and safety professional who has experience in mold remediation procedures. One person in your household should diligently monitor and supervise the remediation and repair process to make sure that work is progressing and completed in a timely fashion. Obtain a written contract that includes estimated completion dates for various stages of the work, and have the contractor develop a written action plan within five business days of accepting the job. Check that the job is progressing on schedule, and if not, follow up.

The following five levels of mold abatement summarized here are discussed in greater detail at the New York

City Department of Health's Web site, located at www. nyc.gov/html/doh/html/epi/moldrpt1.html.

LEVEL I (10 SQUARE FEET OR LESS)

This small infestation would most likely involve a ceiling tile or small section of wallboard. You can clean the mold yourself, but you need to educate yourself on proper clean-up methods, personal protection, and potential health hazards.

- Do not attempt cleaning mold if you suffer from asthma, allergies, or immune disorders.

- Wear gloves, eye protection, and an N95 disposable respirator. (These respirators are available at hardware and home improvement stores.)

- Vacate from your work area any infants less than 12 months old, individuals recovering from recent surgery, anyone with a suppressed immune system, or people with chronic lung diseases such as asthma, severe allergies, emphysema, etc.

- Contaminated materials that cannot be cleaned should be removed from your home in a sealed plastic bag to prevent an infestation in another part of your home. (Check with your local department of health to see if there are any special requirements for the disposal of moldy materials in your city or state. Your local land-fill is typically the proper disposal site.)

- Clean your work area when you're done with a damp cloth or mop.

- Make sure all areas are left dry and visibly free of mold contamination.

LEVEL II (10 TO 30 SQUARE FEET)

This clean-up would most likely involve an area the size of one complete wallboard panel. The recommendations are the same as for Level I, with the added precaution that:

- Moldy materials should be covered with plastic sheets and sealed with tape before any handling or removal of materials. This will contain dust and debris. For example, plastic should be taped over the section of wallboard before it is cut for removal. Once the section is cut, the contaminated section should be placed inside another layer of plastic and sealed with tape before it is removed from your home for disposal.

- When the mold removal is finished, vacuum the work area with an HEPA vacuum (a vacuum fitted with a high-efficiency particulate air filter). Clean the area with a damp cloth or mop.

LEVEL III (30 TO 100 SQUARE FEET)

This infestation would most likely involve patches of mold on several wallboard panels. The recommendations are the same as for Level I and II, with the following added precautions:

- Seal ventilation ducts/grills in the work area and areas directly adjacent with plastic sheeting.

- Vacate *everyone* from your work area until work is completed. Further vacate from adjacent work areas any infants less than 12 months old, individuals recovering from recent surgery, anyone with a suppressed immune system, or people with chronic lung diseases such as asthma, severe allergies, emphysema, etc.

LEVEL IV (GREATER THAN 100 SQUARE FEET)

This infestation would most likely involve entire walls and/or floors (carpeting) that may be thickly coated with mold. The recommendations are the same as for Level I, II, and III, with the following added precautions:

- Every worker must be trained in the handling of hazardous materials and equipped with full-face respirators with high-efficiency particulate air (HEPA) cartridges, with disposable protective clothing covering both head and shoes.

- Make sure workers completely isolate their work area from the rest of your home with sheeting sealed with duct tape, including ventilation ducts/grills, fixtures, and any other openings.

- Make sure workers set up and use a "decontamination room," or a chamber taped off with plastic sheeting. The outside of sealed bags containing contaminated material should be wiped down with a damp cloth or HEPA vacuumed in the decontamination chamber prior to their removal.

- Air monitoring should be conducted prior to moving back into your home to determine if it is fit to reoccupy.

LEVEL V (AIR CONDITIONERS AND HVAC SYSTEMS)

The cooling coils and condensation pans in stand-alone air conditioners and HVAC systems are prime candidates for mold contamination. However, the clean-up of HVAC infestations are not for do-it-yourselfers. While you may clean a small patch of mold growing underneath your stand-alone air conditioner according to the guidelines of a Level I and II infestation, remediation of an HVAC system is best left to the professionals.

The recommendations for a Level V remediation greater than 10 square feet are the same as for all the previous levels, with the following added precautions:

- Shut down the HVAC system prior to remediation.

- Growth-supporting materials that are contaminated, such as the paper on the insulation of interior lined ducts and filters, should be removed and sealed in plastic bags.

- A variety of biocides—broad-spectrum antimicrobial agents designed to prevent the growth of microorganisms—are recommended by HVAC manufacturers for use with HVAC components, such as cooling coils and condensation pans. HVAC manufacturers should be consulted for the products they recommend for use in their systems.

MOLD AND YOUR INSURANCE COMPANY

READ YOUR HOME INSURANCE POLICY

Now you know what you must do to rid your home of mold. But who's going to pay for it? Your insurance company?

Don't count on it.

Policyholders of America (POA), a nonprofit group dedicated to eliminating fraud and bad faith from the insurance claims handling process, says that if you've never done so, now is the time to read your home insurance policy from cover to cover—twice—and take notes.

Under a standard home insurance policy, mold damage—like damage from rust or dry rot—is specifically *excluded* from coverage, unless it's the result of a sudden and accidental water discharge, such as a burst water pipe, blown washing machine hose, or water used to put out a fire.

Typically excluded from standard home insurance policies are damages resulting from:

- Normal wear and tear

- Poor maintenance (you should have replaced the shower grout, but didn't)

- Standing or surface water (unless it's floodwater and you purchased separate flood insurance)

- Construction mistakes or defects (nails accidentally driven into water pipes, or faulty home design)

You need to understand what's covered under your policy (and what's not) so you can accurately report your claim to your insurer. This removes any excuse for the insurer to improperly deny your claim.

Even if you have a legitimate water-damage or mold claim, you may find your policy has additional coverage restrictions in place. These include financial caps (anywhere from $5000 to $100,000) that limit the amount an insurer pays for property damage and liability claims related to fungi, wet or dry rot, or bacterial damage. Liability insurance offers policyholders some financial protection from lawsuits.

HOW TO HANDLE MOLD AND WATER-DAMAGE CLAIMS

When it comes to mold, the learning curve for Texas home owners and their public officials has been swift and steep. Forced to confront the crisis of skyrocketing mold claims head on, the Texas Department of Insurance—with input from insurance industry representatives, consumer groups, builders, lenders, scientists, and mold remediators—has developed guidelines for how to handle mold and water-damage claims.

These suggested practices alone do not address all of the issues, but they serve to improve the processing of water-damage claims resulting in losses from mold infestations. They outline the roles of the insurance industry and the consumer in dealing with these kinds of claims. According to the TDI, once you've identified a potential water-damage or mold claim you should:

- Stop the water leak or flow of water.

- Notify your insurer immediately. If you let any damage fester and don't report it immediately, your claim may be denied. Remember, sudden leaks are covered, but chronic leaks are not.

- Ask what is required of you. Your duties, as outlined in most home insurance policies, may include:
  1. Giving prompt written notice to your insurer of the facts surrounding your claim.
  2. Protecting your property from further damage.
  3. Performing reasonable and necessary repairs to protect your property.
  4. Keeping an accurate record of your repair expenses.

> *Tip:* *Policy provisions require you to provide your company with a written notice of claim, but on most water damage claims your initial contact should be via telephone. Initial contact may be with your insurance agent, a claims office, or the toll-free number included in the policy. Have your policy number available and be prepared to provide information on the extent and severity of the water damage.*

- Make a list of your damaged property and photograph or videotape the damage before making repairs.

- Don't make large structural or permanent repairs. Only make temporary repairs to protect your home and belongings until your insurer has the opportunity to inspect the damage and gives you authorization to make permanent repairs. The insurance company may deny your claim if you make permanent repairs before it inspects the damage.

- Remove standing water and begin drying the area.

> *Note: Be aware that your home insurer's practices may contradict accepted mold prevention procedures if the company prevents you from removing wet building material from your home within 24 to 48 hours of a flood or water intrusion. Make sure you reiterate to your insurer in your telephone conversations and in writing that you need approval as soon as possible to remove water-soaked materials from your home in order to prevent a mold infestation.*

- Remove water-soaked materials.

- Keep removed materials and move them to a secure, dry, and well-ventilated area, or outdoors.

- Protect repairable and undamaged items from further damage.

- Keep an activity log, including a record of all contact with your insurance company. This is *extremely* important. A log not only helps you stay focused and organized, it may play a key part in negotiations with your insurer should you encounter problems with your claim later on.

- Keep all receipts. For personal property claims, you must provide evidence that you bought the replacement items. If you bought materials for temporary repairs, receipts will help you get reimbursed.

- Don't throw away removed or damaged materials until instructed by your insurance company.

- Don't jeopardize your safety.

- Don't exceed your personal financial or physical capabilities.

Note: These suggested policies are not mandatory for insurers and do not amend existing state insurance laws nor the provisions of the insurance contract between you and your insurer.

WHAT TO EXPECT FROM YOUR INSURANCE COMPANY

According to the Texas Department of Insurance, unless there's a major catastrophe where you live, such as a hurricane or flood, your insurer should contact you within 24 hours (one business day) of receiving notice of your claim. At this time, the insurer should share information regarding emergency repairs and mold prevention. If your home has an active leak, your insurer may verify that you've shut off the water. Your insurer may also advise you to contact a qualified professional, such as a plumber, to fix the problem. Although your insurer may provide you with a list of people or companies qualified to do the job, it's your right to select the qualified professional of your choice, even someone who is not on your insurer's list.

Additionally, it is not unreasonable to expect your insurer to:

- Provide the name and contact information of a company representative and advise you that multiple individuals may be involved with the investigation and processing of your claim. However, one insurance company representative should oversee your claim and be available to answer questions.

- Barring a natural disaster, your insurer should send a company representative to your home within 24 to 72 hours of notice of the claim.

- Determine whether your claim is covered and provide an initial estimate of damage within 7 to 14 days after the company representative's initial onsite visit. This initial estimate is subject to change. Within the same time frame, your company should strive to provide you with a written statement confirming or denying coverage.

- Return all phone calls within 24 hours.

Note: *Under most home insurance policies, your insurer is responsible for paying the actual and necessary cost to repair or replace the damaged part of your home with material of "like kind and quality," subject to your limit of liability and all other policy provisions. However, your insurer is not responsible for paying any claims that do not exceed the policy deductible.*

WHAT YOUR INSURER EXPECTS FROM YOU

In order for your insurer to do its job, you must do yours. If you cannot be available to provide information and access to your home, you must provide your insurer with the name and contact information of a responsible person who will do so. You or your representative should be available to allow prompt inspection of the damage to minimize delays in claims processing. Cooperation and complete information is necessary in order to accurately and adequately resolve the claim. Remember, should you have to move out of your home, be sure to provide your insurer with updated contact information so they are able to reach you when necessary.

While the company representative inspecting your home may be your most direct contact with the company, claims processing involves a number of company representatives. Having one person available to deal with your insurer reduces the risk of providing incomplete or inaccurate information, and it helps the claims process proceed smoothly. Written notes should be kept as a record of any requests for additional information or problems encountered during the claims process. For the complete guidelines, visit the Texas Department of Insurance Web site at: www.tdi.state.tx.us/consumer/ moldpub.html.

PROTECT YOURSELF DURING THE CLAIMS PROCESS

Many mold and water-damage claims are reported incorrectly, and your insurer may deny your claim if it is inaccurate. Don't rush when you're filling out the paperwork for your claim.

Your insurer may also require that you fill out a "Proof of Loss" form. Each state varies, but this form is typically sent to policyholders within 15 days after a loss is reported. In most cases, your insurer will ask you to estimate the replacement cost of the household items you lost and the cost of repairing your home. Contractors, catalogs, and retailers are good sources of current price information. But if you don't know the cost, don't guess. Be honest and say that you do not yet know, but make sure you do get bids for replacement. Those bids should include:

- All of the costs necessary to repair and replace property damaged or destroyed with like kind and quality.

- Applicable sales tax, shipment costs, general contractor's fees (should one be required), interior design fee (if applicable), and architectural or engineering fees (if necessary). Your insurer will use this form to decide the value of your claim, so be as detailed as possible. Include photos and receipts. Be sure to keep copies for your records.

During the claims process, your insurer may also require you to submit to an "Examination Under Oath." The Policyholders of America (POA) warns that you must be honest in your sworn statement, but don't volunteer any information that you're not sure is correct. If you don't know something, don't speculate. There's absolutely nothing wrong with saying "I don't know" if you're asked a question outside your scope of expertise.

For example, if you're asked what caused a water leak and you have no idea, say so. Once your insurer has taken your sworn statement, ask for a copy of it.

Your insurer's representative, also known as an adjuster, will prepare an estimate of the cost to repair or replace your home and any personal belongings. Your insurer's offer is usually based on this estimate. It may be much lower than your bid to repair your home and replace your damaged belongings.

At this point you may want to produce, for your insurer, other bids that support your actual bid to perform the work required and document your unsuccessful attempts to get other contractors to perform the work for the amount authorized by your insurer. Once this supporting documentation is obtained, write to your insurer and the adjuster and dispute their estimate. If your insurer's delays are increasing the damage being done to your home or causing other problems—such as worsening health symptoms—make sure you include this information in your letter.

If you receive a check that is woefully inadequate to cover the full scope of the necessary repairs to your home, *do not cash it*. If the insurer has issued you a partial payment, make sure you have it in writing that the check amount is indeed a partial payment and you are awaiting full settlement to complete the necessary repairs. Write your insurer and ask if you should return the check, given that permanent repairs cannot be made for the sum paid (resend your bids and supporting documentation). Don't cash any check if it contains language on the check or in an accompanying letter that indicates the sum paid represents final payment to settle the claim, unless you're satisfied with the settlement figure.

Note: When your insurer pays your claim in full, begin the permanent repairs immediately (assuming those repairs will not jeopardize any ongoing investigation being conducted by your insurer). Don't pocket the money or put it toward anything other than the necessary repairs. Anything else is insurance fraud.

If the claim is only partially paid, you will need to decide whether you should pay the money necessary to make permanent repairs up front. In most cases, that is not economically feasible. Remember, don't exceed your personal financial capabilities.

Your duties when making a mold or water-damage claim are more fully explained at the POA Web site, located at www.policyholdersofamerica.org.

SHOULD YOU MOVE OUT DURING REPAIRS TO YOUR HOME?

Before moving, you should consult your family's physicians. Additionally, when deciding whether relocation is necessary, you and your insurer should consider the following factors:

- Is the home uninhabitable due to significant structural damage?

- Is the mold growing in a light traffic area, such as your garage, or a key living space, such as a kitchen or bedroom?

- Do any members of your household have health symptoms that are aggravated by exposure to mold?

- Is there a time-link relationship between the symptoms and the mold infestation, or can the symptoms be linked to another potential cause, such as the adoption of a new family pet?

If you and your insurer agree that it's necessary for you to relocate during the repairs, you will most likely be granted "additional living expenses" (ALE), as defined in standard home insurance policies. As defined by the TDI, ALE refers to "any necessary and reasonable increase in living expense you incur so that your household can maintain its normal standard of living."

According to TDI guidelines, for typical water-damage claims, it is appropriate for your insurer to:

- Determine if ALE is payable within 10 to 14 days of notice of your claim.

- Provide advance payment for ALE within 24 hours of determination of need.

- Reimburse covered ALE within five business days of receipt of documentation.

- Provide information on ALE provisions of your specific policy, such as how it may be used, and the limits of coverage available under your policy.

- Keep you advised of remaining coverage available under the ALE provisions.

It is your responsibility to monitor your expenses closely and know the limits of your policy. Discuss the timing of recurring bills—such as rent—with your adjuster to ensure that claims processing time is considered. When possible, consider using vendors who can directly bill your insurer.

You should obtain a written action plan from your mold remediator and/or general contractor regarding when repairs will be completed. Monitor the repair progress. You should compare the estimated time you will be out of your home to your coverage limits. Even if you believe your ALE coverage is adequate based on the contractor's estimated completion date, additional damage may be uncovered during the remediation process and the repair time lengthened.

WHAT TO DO WHEN A CLAIM GOES BAD

Most of the time, the claims process proceeds smoothly. However, miscommunication between you and your insurance company's representatives may arise. The best way to avoid this problem is to document all your conversations with and activities by your insurer, including dates, names of company representatives, dates when requests for additional information were given to you, and dates the additional information was provided.

Documenting all conversations with written notes will reduce the risk of misunderstandings between you and your insurer. In the event a misunderstanding cannot be resolved, this documented record will make it easier for insurance company officials or your state Department of Insurance (DOI) to assist you in resolving your complaint.

If you're having a problem with your insurer's representative, be persistent. Request to speak to the representative's manager, and continue up the chain of command as necessary. If you cannot resolve the dispute directly with your insurer, file a written complaint with your state DOI. This complaint will trigger an investigation into the matter. To find the contact information for your state DOI, see Chapter 8.

But what if the problem seems to be more than a simple miscommunication between you and your insurer? Be aware that every state has laws that prohibit unfair, discriminatory, or deceptive insurance practices. These laws define what is acceptable conduct in the insurance industry and cover everything from sales practices to policy cancellation. Generally speaking, an insurer:

- Must acknowledge your claim (some states have deadlines, such as 15 days)

- Must process your claim promptly (otherwise, your insurer could endlessly avoid paying you by saying your claim is still under investigation)

- Must not delay processing your claim by requiring unnecessary or repetitive "proof-of-loss" forms

- Must not refuse or delay claims without a valid reason

A failure to adhere to these practices may constitute what is known as "bad faith."

Note: Denying benefits, delaying payments, and paying less than what is owed are examples of bad faith on the part of the insurer. An insurer is obligated to thoroughly and promptly investigate all claims and must inquire into all the issues that might support a policyholder's claim. In some states, bad faith exposes the insurer to fines well in excess of the policy limits or punitive damages.

According to Policyholders of America, here are some practices that may give rise to a definition of bad faith:

- Wrongful denial of claim.

- Unreasonable delay in paying benefits

- Unreasonable cancellation of the policy

- Failure to conduct a reasonable investigation

- Unreasonable demand on the policyholder to contribute to a settlement

- Refusal to diligently pursue post-trial remedies

- Failure to keep the policyholder informed of significant developments

- Failure to advise the insured of a right to arbitrate

POA cautions that whoever is going to assume the "point person" responsibilities for dealing with the day-to-day issues of any claim problems must have the time and energy available to devote to establishing and recovering any money or benefits due. This can sometimes be extremely time-consuming. Whether you or another family member assumes this role, it helps to understand the options available to you to settle your claim. These options are:

- The right to demand an appraisal

- Recourse to a public adjuster

- Legal remedies

APPRAISAL

Many policies contain language giving both the insurer and the policyholder the right to demand the "appraisal process." This process is only applicable if coverage has been accepted (not denied) and the dispute revolves around the cost to repair or replace. It cannot address personal injuries or questions of coverage.

You can request an appraisal by notifying your insurer in writing. Then you and your insurer each selects an independent appraiser. Neither appraiser should have an existing business or personal relationship with either party involved, otherwise the decision may be overturned in court. The two appraisers must agree on an "umpire," or a judge will appoint one. If the appraisers are unable to agree on the amount of damage, they will submit their differences to the umpire. The umpire should also be independent and should not have any sort of business or personal relationship with either side.

Ultimately, any two of the three reaching an agreement on the amount of damage constitutes an award, which is binding in most states. A thorough appraisal may cost the policyholder between $15,000 and $25,000. The cost of the umpire is split equally between you and your insurer.

PUBLIC ADJUSTER

Public adjusters usually are licensed by the Department of Insurance in the state in which they operate. They can address coverage issues (if a legitimate claim is denied, they may be able to prove coverage exists) and help prove the actual costs of repair or replacement. A public adjuster cannot seek any recovery for a personal injury claim. Public adjusters typically charge between 10 and 30 percent of the recovery. Some work on an hourly basis. If a public adjuster is retained, be sure to have a plan outlined should the adjuster be unable to successfully recover money due you. If a lawyer is eventually retained, you do not want to owe fees to both a public adjuster and an attorney.

LEGAL REMEDIES

This is usually the most expensive and time-consuming option, but is usually considered best if bad faith is involved or if the insurer can be held accountable for personal injuries arising out of its actions or inactions. You can expect to pay an attorney between 33 to 45 percent of any settlement, depending upon whether out-of-pocket expenses are absorbed by the attorney.

CHECKLIST: MAKING A MOLD OR WATER-DAMAGE CLAIM

Check all that apply to your situation.

☐ I have stopped the water leak or flow of water.

☐ I have notified my home insurer.

☐ I have made a list of my damaged property and photographed or videotaped the damage before making repairs.

☐ I am protecting my property from further damage.

☐ I have removed standing water and I'm drying the area.

☐ I have removed water-soaked materials and I'm keeping them in a secure, dry, and well-ventilated area, or outdoors until my insurer instructs me to dispose of them.

☐ I'm keeping all receipts and making an activity log of all contact with my home insurer.

CHAPTER 7

THIS MOLD HOUSE: HOW TO AVOID A REAL ESTATE NIGHTMARE

MOLD MONEY PIT?

You're not alone if you believe that owning your own home is one of the best (as well as biggest) investments you'll ever make. In a September 2002 survey conducted by mortgage giant Fannie Mae, 70 percent of Americans say that they believe buying a home is a safe and smart investment, compared with 38 percent of those polled who say that an IRA or 401K plan is a "safe investment with a lot of potential," and just 10 percent who feel the same way about stocks.

In fact, those polled say the investment aspect of buying a home is often more of a reason to buy than either the size or location of a particular house, which is second only to safety (65 percent) as the most important aspect of buying a home. Home owners nationwide are pouring about $200 billion into home improvement products in order to protect and enhance the investment in their homes.

However, environmental hazards—whether manmade (asbestos insulation and lead-based paint) or naturally occurring (radon, pests, mold)—can cause significant depreciation in the value of your home due to actual damage or the potential for damage to either your home or its occupants. Additionally, if environmental hazards are detected, but not disclosed, they may spark lawsuits that can drain you both financially and emotionally for years to come—even if you no longer own the property!

Take the case of Keith and Debbie Leggett of Peabody, Massachusetts. They are being sued by John and Dawn O'Neil of Merrimack, New Hampshire, who moved out of their home in 2001 after family members began coughing up blood and air-quality experts discovered mold in the O'Neils' attic. The lawsuit alleges that the Leggetts either knew or should have known about the mold when they sold the house to the O'Neils in 1998. The Leggetts deny all claims, including that the home had mold in it when they sold it.

So the Leggetts are being sued for problems with a property they no longer own, and the O'Neils are making mortgage payments on a house in which they can't live—or sell. To complicate matters further, the O'Neils' home insurance policy *doesn't cover any of the damage*. Remember, home insurers consider mold a home maintenance problem and will not pay for mold-related damages unless they are the result of a sudden and accidental discharge of water. It's cases such as this one that really worry home buyers, home sellers, and real estate professionals. With no established standards for acceptable levels of indoor mold, how does anyone buy or sell buildings with any degree of confidence that the property they are purchasing, selling, or brokering will not suddenly turn into a "toxic" mold money pit?

The Mold Working Group of the National Association of Realtors(NAR) is in the process of addressing this issue. They conclude in their April 2002 report:

> "While some studies and experiences conclude that some molds, at some concentrations, at some exposure levels for some people, may have adverse health effects, the science on the health effects of mold remains relatively undeveloped."

The report recommends a proposed amendment to NAR's property condition disclosure policy to include "water intrusion" as well as "known existing or past mold presence (*other than that which is known to not adversely affect the property or its occupants*)," in addition to disclosures relating to hazardous materials such as asbestos, lead-based paint, radon, and underground storage tanks.

Because federal and state protocols on mold exposure in residential structures range from minimal to nonexistent, home buyers often look to third parties—such as insurers, inspectors, contractors, and realtors—to pay for mold remediation, says Robert Brand, a California general contractor who works as a consultant on mold litigation avoidance strategies. However, the threat of third-party litigation shouldn't paralyze you to the point of preventing you from buying or selling a home. The tips below can help you focus on the task at hand—buying or selling a home— without succumbing to any mold hype or hysteria.

TIPS FOR HOME BUYERS

Demand Full Disclosure

Insist that the sellers tell you about all prior water damage, water intrusion, structural repairs, any testing done for mold, or any mold-abatement procedures. State laws regarding full disclosure of mold are only now starting to appear. Even if your state doesn't require full disclosure of water intrusion or damage caused by water and/or mold, make sure your real estate agent adds such language to your real estate contract. If the sellers won't sign it, that's a red flag. Be prepared to walk away from the deal.

Note: Do you have a clue about your dream home's past insurance claims? Your insurer does. Ninety percent of home insurers subscribe to CLUE, which stands for Comprehensive Loss Underwriting Exchange, a database of home owners' claims histories.

When you apply for home insurance, your insurer requests a CLUE report to determine whether you, the buyer, or the home seller have filed any claims during the past five years and whether you and the property you're *interested in buying are good insurance risks—if not, you may be denied coverage.*

If you are simply curious about your home's history, you can order a copy from ChoicePoint, the company that owns the CLUE database. Unfortunately, you can't order a CLUE report if you are not the home owner. Prospective buyers aren't allowed to request a CLUE report for a home they want to purchase, but there's nothing stopping you from asking the home owners to provide you with a copy as a condition of the sale. You can order a copy of your CLUE report for $12.95 by calling (866) 527-2600. Choice-Point also makes it possible for you to access your CLUE report via the Internet at its Web site located at www.choicetrust.com.

Inspect. Really Inspect

Make sure you spend as much time poking around your dream home's attic and basement as you do its kitchen, bathrooms, and bedrooms. It also pays to schedule at least one visit to the home during—or just after—a prolonged or heavy rain. Look for leaky windows; water seepage; staining or discoloration under windows or on ceilings and walls, including baseboards; and pay close attention to any smell of mold or mildew.

Additionally, hire an expert to conduct a thorough home inspection prior to closing. Most qualified home inspectors have experience in identifying signs of previous water damage. However, prior to hiring, it doesn't hurt to ask the inspector to detail his or her experience with detecting mold on a premises.

Analyze Inspection Results

If the inspection turns up any red flags, now is the time to consult with the real estate agent or owner. In addition to asking for the CLUE report on the property (see box on page 86), you can also ask for any documentation of previous repairs. You can also search the building permit office's records for past repairs.

If you're still uneasy about the property, now is the time to walk away. However, if the seller does disclose a problem and you have reviewed the records and everything seems in order, see if the seller will work with you to assess current risks. At this point you may want to hire a microbial expert to further inspect, but avoid unnecessary air sampling. It's expensive ($1000 or more) and there's no way to test every square inch of a house. Remember, no qualified professional will guarantee that a home is mold-free, because there is no such thing: All homes contain some mold. Also, while the seller may agree to an inspection by a microbial expert, he or she is most likely not going to allow the expert to open up ceilings and walls or perform any other invasive procedures.

Negotiate

If the seller has been nothing less than up front and honest with you about prior water damage or mold problems, and you're as satisfied as you can be about the home's current condition—but you're still concerned about a recurring infestation—see if the seller is willing to assume part of any financial burden (within reasonable limits) should future contamination occur.

TIPS FOR HOME SELLERS

Repair Mold-Related and/or Water Damage

Even before you put your home on the market, make sure you've taken all the steps necessary to fix any damage related to water intrusion and/or mold infestation. Don't slap a coat of paint over stained, moldy wallboard. This cosmetic quick "fix" is short-lived and does nothing to address the underlying problem.

If the infestation is more than you can handle by yourself, hire a professional to guide you through the remediation process. Think twice if you're tempted to put off fixing a leaky basement window or investigating the warped floor in your bathroom. If a major mold problem is uncovered after the sale, you could very well be held liable for the repairs, as well as sued for damages.

Document Your Repairs

For anything other than a small infestation that you've completely cleaned yourself, document all repairs of any damage related to water intrusion and/or mold infestation. Keep all your receipts and make sure the professionals involved provide you with a detailed account of their work.

Disclose Everything

What the new home owners don't know that you failed to tell them can hurt both of you (and potentially your realtor) big-time. If you're not sure whether you should disclose a seemingly small problem such as a briefly recurring patch of mildew on your bathroom wallpaper that you finally cleaned and replaced, go ahead and tell the buyers anyway. You don't want any surprises at the closing table or later on, when you no longer own the home

Negotiate

What if there's been mold or water damage in the past that has been remediated but the buyer's inspector detects residual levels of contamination? Or what if the inspector gives the house an all clear but the buyers are still concerned about mold returning at a future date? Does this mean you have to kiss your sale good-bye?

Certainly not! If you've been up front with the buyer and you're willing to assume partial cost for possible future repairs related to the original mold or water problem, then the buyer may very well feel secure enough to close the deal.

However, you must be financially able to uphold your end of the bargain should an infestation or reinfestation surface. You must also set limits to what you're willing to pay for future repairs and under what circumstances. Don't sign a blank check.

For that matter, don't sign anything until your attorney reviews all agreements prior to signing.

PAST HOME INSURANCE CLAIMS CAN HAUNT YOU

Just picture it: You're days away from closing on a new home, you've secured your financing, packed up your belongings, and now all that's left is a phone call to your insurance agent to take out a home insurance policy. Then the nightmare begins. You find out your dream home is uninsurable because your insurance company says there is a history of home insurance claims by the previous owner.

Despite home inspections and real estate disclosures required by law, the unthinkable does happen. There are properties with a past history of claims that are virtually uninsurable. And the really scary part is that buyers (and sometimes sellers) are often the last to know.

How do previous claims on a house you don't yet own wind up haunting you? A typical example goes like this: The home owner discovers a leaky bathroom faucet and calls his insurance agent to discuss whether he should file a claim on his home insurance policy. Since the policy has a $500 deductible, he decides to repair it himself and skips filing a claim. During the sale of the house, the home owner discloses to you a previous claim for a burst water pipe in his basement for which his insurer paid, but he doesn't bother to mention the leaky faucet. After all, it is repaired and he spent his own money to fix it. But when you go to purchase a policy for this home, you're denied based on the fact that the home has had *two* claims in the past three years: the burst pipe *and* the leaky faucet.

What has happened is that the home owner's insurer opened a claim file on the leaky faucet as soon as he called and then later marked it "closed, with no payment" when he decided to fix the leak himself. Insurers say it is standard procedure to record such telephone inquiries in this manner. However, these "closed, with no payment" files show up as claims in the CLUE database.

Note: CLUE's database tracks 27 "causes of loss" showing why a claim was submitted to a property/casualty insurer for payment, including: contamination, damage to property of others, dog bite, earthquake, fire, flood, freezing water, hail, lightning, medical payment, slip/fall, smoke, theft/burglary, vandalism, water damage, and wind.

But CLUE reports don't just identify the negatives, says Richard Collier, vice president of ChoicePoint, the company that owns the CLUE database. Buyers can also learn about positive attributes of their potential new home.

"If you're buying an older home and the roof was replaced because of storm damage, you may be very happy knowing you are getting a newer roof," he says. Home insurers have relied on information from CLUE's property and casualty database (there is also one for auto claims) since its launch in 1992. Originally, insurers used it as a background check on applicants to ferret out a pattern of fraudulent claims, according to Jeanne Salvatore, vice president of consumer affairs at the Insurance Information Institute. "What's new is that insurers are now taking a look at individual structures to see if there have been a lot of claims made on the property itself," she says.

Just as previous claims on your auto insurance policy will hike your rates or perhaps cause an insurer to refuse to renew your policy, previous claims on your home insurance policy can affect your ability to obtain coverage on your new home, or at least cause the premiums to double, even triple. Texas real estate broker Karen Wilson, who had an expensive mold claim on a previous Texas home, was aghast to learn that her policy on a brand new home was going to skyrocket from $1100 annually to $2900—all because her insurer learned of her prior water-damage claim on a house she didn't even own anymore.

Not only does CLUE alert insurers to properties that carry potentially more risk than they are willing to assume, but it also gives consumers another tool to make good purchasing decisions. "By having a home's claims history, the buyers have the information they need to confirm if all the necessary repairs were done properly," says Salvatore. "Or if the home has been burglarized in the past, the buyers can check to see if the house is now secure. Do the alarms work? Have new locks been installed? If the answer is no, the buyer can rethink his or her decision to proceed with the purchase, or negotiate a lower price."

The use of CLUE by insurers shouldn't be construed as negative, says Collier. "People fall in love with certain houses and they're upset when they can't get them insured. But it's better to find out before they sign on the dotted line that there are problems rather than to wind up with a nightmare later on."

SHOPPING FOR HOME INSURANCE PRIOR TO CLOSING

It pays to educate yourself about home insurance when you're seeking affordable coverage for your home. Here are some ways you can help yourself:

- *Find out the rules regarding home insurance renewals in your state.* Some states exercise control over when an insurer can refuse to renew your policy. In Texas, for example, an insurer can't refuse to renew your home insurance policy unless you've made three non-weather-related claims within the past three years. To find the contact information for your state department of insurance, see Chapter 8.

- *Consider paying for small losses out of your own pocket.* Insurers take notice of customers who submit too many small claims. If someone breaks into your house and steals your new stereo that you bought for $400, it might just be better to go out and buy a new one at your own expense, particularly if you've had a claim or two within the past three years.

  Think twice before you call your agent or insurance company. If you're considering filing a claim but aren't sure, wait to make that call. The minute your insurer's customer service representative types in your name in order to log your call, the insurer has opened up a file on you that will be tracked through its computer system.

- *Shop around for coverage.* If your insurer denies you a policy based on previous claims or the rates are simply unaffordable, don't get discouraged. You should obtain quotes from at least three other insurers so you can compare premiums and coverage options. If you can't get a policy from a standard insurer, try a "Lloyd's company"—an insurance company based on

Lloyd's of London, an insurer composed of many different "syndicates," each specializing in insuring a particular risk. Additionally, check to see if your state offers Fair Access to Insurance Requirements plans. FAIR plans were created in the late 1960s to make property insurance more readily available to people who can't obtain it from private insurers because their property is considered "high risk."

- *Raise your deductible and consolidate insurers.* In order to save 10 to 20 percent on your home insurance premium, consider raising your deductible from $250 to $500 or even to $1000 if you can afford it. Also, some insurers will extend you a discount if you insure both your auto and home with them.

- *Check your credit record.* In addition to using your past claims history, insurers will use your credit score to help them decide whether to issue you an auto or home insurance policy, where allowed by state law. In Texas, for example, Allstate Insurance Co. stopped selling new home insurance policies in 2002 to Texas consumers who rank in the bottom three tiers of the insurer's five-tier credit scoring system.

  Additionally, Allstate is not selling home insurance in Texas to any of its existing customers who have low credit scores if they have also filed any claims within the past three years.

You should order a copy of your credit record periodically to ensure it doesn't contain mistakes that could prevent you from obtaining a home insurance policy or that will cause your insurer to raise your premiums.

CHECKLIST: SHOPPING FOR HOME INSURANCE PRIOR TO CLOSING

Check all that apply to your situation.

- ☐ I have educated myself about relevant home insurance regulations in my state.

- ☐ I have shopped around for home insurance coverage.

- ☐ I have considered paying for small losses out of my own pocket.

- ☐ I have raised my home insurance deductible and consolidated insurers.

- ☐ I have checked my credit record.

- ☐ I have checked my own home's CLUE report and/or asked the sellers for a CLUE report on the home I'm thinking of buying.

PART III

HELP FOR HOME OWNERS

CHAPTER 8

WHERE TO TURN FOR HELP

Dealing with a mold infestation may be hazardous to your health. Even if you have no allergic symptoms to the mold, the detergents and disinfectants you'll need to rid your home of mold can be harmful if used improperly. Your best bet for a successful outcome to your mold problem is to seek help and/or information from *reliable* sources. You need to identify people who can legitimately help you without scaring you or conning you into spending money on unnecessary tests and services.

Many states are currently considering legislation that would set basic standards for mold remediators, but by and large, anyone who wants to call him- or herself a mold abatement specialist or remediator may do so. Before you hire anyone to work on your home, seek out other home owners who have experience in mold remediation and selecting contractors. Additionally, contact your local Better Business Bureau to learn whether any of the remediators or contractors you're considering have had any complaints filed against them.

Note: The misinformation, hype, and hysteria about mold—as well as a few sizable jury awards—have spawned a cottage industry involved in mold fraud. The worst? Con artists posing as professional mold remediators who convince you to move out of your house because of mold and then proceed to hose down the inside of your house—drapes, furniture, bedding, carpets—and then close up your windows and turn up the heat in order to produce mold. This is known as "cooking the house." This scam is sometimes done in collusion with the home owner in order to defraud the home owner's insurance company.

Fortunately, there are more places to seek solid information on the topic of mold than there were even just two years ago. One of the first places you can start your search is your state health department.

The list following is current as this book goes to print.

STATE DEPARTMENTS OF HEALTH

If you have access to the Internet—either at home or at your public library—you can often find in-depth information about the potential health problems associated with mold exposure at your health department's Web site. Many health departments produce fact sheets that you may order online or obtain by calling the departments directly.

Alabama Department of Public Health
Web site: www.adph.org/Default.asp?bhcp=1
Phone: (334) 206-5200

Alaska Health and Social Services
Web site: www.health.hss.state.ak.us/
Phone: (907) 465-3030

Arizona Department of Health Services
Web site: www.hs.state.az.us/
Phone: (602) 542-1000

Arkansas Department of Health
Web site: www.healthyarkansas.com/
Phone: (501) 661-2000

California Department of Health Services
Web site: www.dhs.cahwnet.gov/
Phone: (916) 445-4171

**Colorado Department of Public Health
and Environment**
Web site: www.cdphe.state.co.us/cdphehom.asp
Phone: (303) 692-2035

Connecticut Department of Public Health
Web site: www.dph.state.ct.us/
Phone: (860) 509-8000

Florida Department of Health
Web site: www.doh.state.fl.us/
Phone: (850) 245-4443

Georgia Division of Public Health
Web site: www.ph.dhr.state.ga.us/
Phone: (404) 657-2700

Hawaii Department of Public Health
Web site: www.hawaii.gov/health/
Phone: (808) 586-4400 or (808) 586-4442

Idaho Department of Health and Welfare
Web site: www.state.id.us/dhw/health/
Phone: (208) 334-5500

Illinois Department of Public Health
Web site: www.idph.state.il.us/home.htm
Phone: (217) 782-4977

Indiana Department of Public Health
Web site: www.in.gov/isdh/index.htm
Phone: (317) 233-8000

Iowa Department of Public Health
Web site: www.idph.state.ia.us/
Phone: (515) 281-5787

Kansas Department of Health and Environment
Web site: www.kdhe.state.ks.us/health/index.html
Phone: (785) 296-1343

Kentucky Department of Health
Web site: publichealth.state.ky.us/
Phone: (502) 564-7398

Louisiana Department of Health and Hospitals
Web site: www.dhh.state.la.us/
Phone: (225) 342-9500

Maine Bureau of Health
Web site: www.state.me.us/dhs/boh/index.htm
Phone: (207) 287-8016

Maryland Department of Health and Mental Hygiene
Web site: www.dhmh.state.md.us/
Phone toll free: (877) 463-3464

Massachusetts Department of Public Health
Web site: www.state.ma.us/dph/dphhome.htm
Phone: (617) 624-6000

Michigan Department of Community Health
Web site: www.michigan.gov/mdch
Phone: (517) 373-3500

Mississippi State Department of Health
Web site: www.msdh.state.ms.us/msdhsite/index.cfm
Phone: (601) 576-7400

Missouri Department of Health and Senior Services
Web site: www.health.state.mo.us/
Phone: (573) 751-6400

**Montana Department of Public Health
and Human Services**
Web site: www.dphhs.state.mt.us/
Phone: (406) 444-4540

Nebraska Health and Human Services
Web site: www.hhs.state.ne.us/
Phone: (402) 471-2306

Nevada State Health Division
Web site: www.health2k.state.nv.us/
Phone: (775) 684-4200

**New Hampshire Department of Health
and Human Services**
Web site:
www.dhhs.state.nh.us/DHHS/DHHS_SITE/default.htm
Phone: (603) 271-4501
Phone toll free: (800) 852-3345 (ext. 4501)

**New Jersey Department of Health
and Senior Services**
Web site: www.state.nj.us/health/
Phone: (609) 292-4993

New York State Department of Health
Web site: www.health.state.ny.us/home.html
Phone toll free: (800) 458-1158

**North Carolina Department of Health
and Human Services**
Web site: www.dhhs.state.nc.us/
Phone: (919) 733-2870

North Dakota Department of Health
Web site: www.health.state.nd.us/
Phone toll free: (888) 246-2675

Ohio Department of Health
Web site: www.odh.state.oh.us/
Phone: (614) 466-3543

Oklahoma State Department of Health
Web site: www.health.state.ok.us/
Phone: (405) 271-5600

Oregon Department of Human Services
Web site: www.ohd.hr.state.or.us/
Phone: (503) 731-4000

Pennsylvania Department of Health
Web site:
www.webserver.health.state.pa.us/ health/site/
Phone toll free: (800) 222-0989

Rhode Island Department of Health
Web site: www.health.state.ri.us/
Phone: (401) 222-2231

**South Carolina Department of Health
and Human Services**
Web site: www.dhhs.state.sc.us/
Phone: (803) 898-2500

South Dakota Department of Health
Web site: www.state.sd.us/doh/index.htm
Phone: (605) 773-3361
Phone toll free: (800) 738-2301

Tennessee Department of Health
Web site: www.state.tn.us/health/
Phone: (615) 741-3111

Texas Department of Health
Web site: www.tdh.state.tx.us/
Phone: (512) 458-7111
Phone toll free: (888) 963-7111

Utah Department of Health
Web site: www.hlunix.hl.state.ut.us/
Phone: (801) 538-6101

Vermont Department of Health
Web site: www.healthyvermonters.info/
Phone: (802) 863-7200
Phone toll free: (800) 464-4343

Virginia Department of Health
Web site: www.vdh.state.va.us/
Phone: (804) 786-1763

Washington State Department of Health
Web site: www.doh.wa.gov/
Phone toll free: (800) 525-0127
(in state only)

**West Virginia Department of Health
and Human Resources**
Web site: www.wvdhhr.org/
Phone: (304) 558-0684

**Wisconsin Department of Health
and Family Services**
Web site: www.dhfs.state.wi.us/
Phone: (608) 266-1865

Wyoming Department of Health
Web site:
www.wdhfs.state.wy.us/WDH/index.htm
Phone: (307) 777-7123

STATE DEPARTMENTS OF INSURANCE

Your state department of insurance (DOI) may also provide valuable information on what to do when you have a mold infestation, as well as how to make a water-damage or mold claim on your home insurance policy. You will also want to contact your DOI if you encounter problems with your claim that you and your home insurer cannot resolve (see Chapter 6).

Many DOIs have complaint forms posted on their Web sites that you can fill out and submit online. A completed complaint form will trigger an investigation into your problem. The list below is current as this book goes to print.

Alabama Department of Insurance
Web site: www.aldoi.org/
Phone: (334) 269-3550

Alaska Division of Insurance
Web site: www.dced.state.ak.us/insurance/
Phone: (907) 465-2515

Arizona Department of Insurance
Web site: www.state.az.us/id/
Phone toll free: (800) 325-2548 (in state only)

Arkansas Insurance Department
Web site: www.state.ar.us/insurance/
Phone: (501) 371-2600

California Department of Insurance
Web site: www.insurance.ca.gov/docs/index.html
Phone: (213) 897-8921

Colorado Division of Insurance
Web site: www.dora.state.co.us/insurance/
Phone: (303) 894-7499
Phone toll free: (800) 930-3745 (in state only)

Connecticut Insurance Department
Web site: www.state.ct.us/cid/
Phone: (860) 297-3800
Phone toll free: (800) 203-3447

Delaware Insurance Department
Web site: www.state.de.us/inscom/
Phone: (302) 739-4251

**District of Columbia Department
of Insurance and Securities Regulation**
Web site: www.disr.washingtondc.gov/main.shtm
Phone: (202) 727-8000

Florida Department of Insurance
Web site: www.doi.state.fl.us/
Phone toll free: (800) 342-2762 (in state only)

Georgia Insurance and Safety Fire Department
Web site: www.inscomm.state.ga.us/
Phone: (404) 656-2056

**Hawaii Department of Commerce
and Consumer Affairs**
Web site: www.state.hi.us/dcca/ins/
Phone: (808) 586-2790

Idaho Department of Insurance
Web site: www.doi.state.id.us/
Phone: (208) 334-4250
Phone toll free: (800) 721-3272

Illinois Department of Insurance
Web site: www.ins.state.il.us/
Phone: (217) 782-4515
Phone toll free: (866) 445-5364
(Consumer assistance hotline, in state only)

Indiana Department of Insurance
Web site: www.state.in.us/idoi/
Phone: (317) 232-2385

Iowa Insurance Division
Web site: www.iid.state.ia.us/
Phone: (515) 281-5705
Phone toll free: (877) 955-1212
(in state only)

Kansas Insurance Commissioner
Web site: www.ksinsurance.org/
Phone: (785) 296-3071

Phone toll free: (800) 432-2484
(Consumer assistance hotline)
Phone: Wichita (316) 337-6010
Phone toll free: Wichita hotline (800) 860-5260

Kentucky Department of Insurance
Web site: www.doi.state.ky.us/kentucky/
Phone: (502) 564-3630
Phone toll free: (800) 595-6053

Louisiana Department of Insurance
Web site: www.ldi.ldi.state.la.us/
Phone: (225) 342-5900
Phone toll free: (800) 259-5300 or
(800) 259-5301 (in-state only)

Maine Bureau of Insurance
Web site:
www.state.me.us/pfr/ins/ins_index.htm
Phone: (207) 624-8475
Phone toll free: (800) 300-5000 (in state only)

Maryland Insurance Administration
Web site: www.mdinsurance.state.md.us/
Phone: (410) 468-2000
Phone toll free: (800) 492-6116

Massachusetts Division of Insurance
Web site: www.state.ma.us/doi/
Phone: (617) 521-7794

Michigan Department of Consumer and Industry Services
Web site: www.michigan.gov/cis
Phone: (517) 373-0220
Phone toll free: (877) 999-6442

Minnesota Department of Commerce
Web site: www.commerce.state.mn.us/
Phone: (651) 297-7161

Missouri Department of Insurance
Web site: www.insurance.state.mo.us/
Phone toll free: (800) 726-7390 (Consumer hotline)
Phone: Jefferson City (573) 751-2640
Phone: Kansas City (816) 889-2381
Phone: St. Louis (314) 340-6830

Mississippi Department of Insurance
Web site: www.doi.state.ms.us/
Phone: (601) 359-2453
Phone toll free: (800) 562-2957 (in state only)

Montana State Auditor's Office
Web site: www.discoveringmontana.com/sao/
Phone: (406) 444-2040
Phone toll free: (800) 332-6148

Nebraska Department of Insurance
Web site: www.nol.org/home/NDOI/
Phone: (402) 471-2201

Nevada Division of Insurance
Web site: www.doi.state.nv.us/
Phone: Carson City (775) 687-4270
Phone: Las Vegas (702) 486-4009

New Hampshire Insurance Department
Web site: www.state.nh.us/insurance/
Phone: (603) 271-2261
Phone toll free: (800) 852-3416

New Jersey Department of Banking and Insurance
Web site: www.state.nj.us/dobi/index.shtml
Phone: (609) 292-5360

New Mexico Insurance Division
Web site: www.nmprc.state.nm.us/inshm.htm
Phone: (505) 827-4601
Phone toll free: (800) 947-4722 (in state only)

New York State Insurance Department
Web site: www.ins.state.ny.us/nyins.htm
Phone toll free: (800) 342-3736
(Consumer services, in state only)
Phone: Albany (800) 323-3736 (toll free)
or (518) 474-6600
Phone: Buffalo (716) 847-7618
Phone: Long Island (Mineola) (516) 248-5886
Phone: New York City (212) 480-6400
Phone: Oneonta (607) 433-0108
Phone: Rochester (716) 325-1857
Phone: Syracuse (315) 423-1102

North Carolina Department of Insurance
Web site: www.ncdoi.com/
Phone: (919) 733-2032
Phone toll free: (800) 546-5664

North Dakota Department of Insurance
Web site: www.state.nd.us/ndins/
Phone: (701) 328-2440

Ohio Department of Insurance
Web site: www.ohioinsurance.gov/
Phone: (614) 644-2658
Phone toll free: (800) 686-1526
(Consumer hotline)

Oklahoma Insurance Department
Web site: www.oid.state.ok.us/
Phone: (405) 521-2686

Oregon Insurance Division
Web site:
www.cbs.state.or.us/external/ins/index.html
Phone: (503) 947-7980

Pennsylvania Insurance Department
Web site: www.insurance.state.pa.us/
Phone toll free: (877) 881-6388 (in state only)
Phone: Erie Regional Office (814) 871-4466
Phone: Philadelphia Regional Office (215) 560-2630
Phone: Pittsburgh Regional Office (412) 565-5020

Rhode Island Insurance Division
Web site: www.dbr.state.ri.us/insurance.html
Phone: (401) 222-2223

South Carolina Department of Insurance
Web site: www.doi.state.sc.us/
Phone: (803) 737-6160

South Dakota Division of Insurance
Web site: www.state.sd.us/dcr/insurance/
Phone: (605) 773-3563

Tennessee Insurance Division
Web site:
www.state.tn.us/commerce/insurdiv.html
Phone: (615) 741-2241

Texas Department of Insurance
Web site: www.tdi.state.tx.us/
Phone: (512) 463-6464

Utah Insurance Department
Web site: www.insurance.state.ut.us/
Phone: (801) 538-3800

Virginia Bureau of Insurance
Web site: www.state.va.us/scc/division/boi/index.htm
Phone: (804) 371-9741
Phone toll free: (800) 552-7945 (in state only)

Vermont Department of Banking, Insurance, Securities & Health Care Administration
Web site: www.bishca.state.vt.us/
Phone: (802) 828-3301

Washington State Department of Insurance
Web site: www.insurance.wa.gov/shibahelpline.htm
Phone toll free: (800) 562-6900 (in state only)

West Virginia Insurance Commission
Web site: www.state.wv.us/insurance/
Phone: (304) 558-3354
Phone toll free: (800) 642-9004 (in state only)

Wisconsin Office of Insurance
Web site: www.oci.wi.gov/oci_home.htm
Phone: (608) 266-3585
Phone toll free: (800) 236-8517 (in state only)

Wyoming Insurance Department
Web site: www.insurance.state.wy.us/
Phone: (307) 777-7401

POLICYHOLDERS OF AMERICA

Founded by Melinda Ballard after winning her bad faith lawsuit against Farmers Insurance Group, Policyholders of America (POA) is a nonpartisan nonprofit organization dedicated to guiding insurance policyholders through the claims process and eradicating fraud and bad faith from that process. POA also endorses and supports political candidates who are tough consumer advocates. At $100 annually ($250 if you're an attorney or other professional), membership in POA is not for everybody. However, membership does allow you access to the secure part of POA's Web site, which includes an extensive legal and medical library. As a member, you can e-mail POA questions and the organization will forward them to its experts—ranging from attorneys who specialize in bad faith insurance cases to medical doctors and everything in between. POA will then e-mail you their expert's reply.

There are also public sections of POA's Web site, as well as free limited-time passes to gain access to protected information. The free public information includes a list of POA-approved contractors, in addition to information on making an insurance claim and what constitutes insurance bad faith.

LEGISLATIVE HELP

Just a few years ago, there were no laws that specifically addressed mold. Today, more than a dozen states have passed legislation aimed at protecting consumers by setting mold exposure guidelines and/or limiting insurance companies' liability for mold cleanup. A list of these states may be found at the POA Web site, at www.policy holdersofamerica.org/legislate_state_by_state.html. More states will certainly follow suit.

Although Texas is a hotbed for proposed mold legislation as this book goes to print, California is actually the first state in the nation to begin regulating the fungus. Effective January 1, 2002, the state's Toxic Mold Protection Act directs the California Department of Health Services to develop standards for mold exposure. The bill also will eventually require landlords and home owners to disclose the presence of mold when selling buildings.

There may one day be a federal law as well. In 2002, U.S. Rep. John Conyers (D-Michigan) introduced the U.S. Toxic Mold Safety and Protection Act, legislation aimed at helping protect consumers from toxic mold and forcing insurers to slash rising home insurance premiums. The bill was not acted upon, but it was reintroduced to the 108th Congress in 2003.

The U.S. Toxic Mold Safety and Protection Act calls for establishment of an insurance pool to cover the costs associated with toxic mold cleanup. It also calls for the Environmental Protection Agency to establish guidelines on the "acceptable" levels of toxic mold in your home, to establish professional standards for mold inspectors and remediators, and to set up a national database of homes that are infested with "toxic" mold.

Additionally, it called for the establishment of an insurance pool that would cover the costs associated with toxic mold cleanup if you opt to purchase the additional coverage from the pool. The self-funded insurance pool would mimic the current flood insurance system and take the liability of toxic mold cleanup off insurers, unless it is due to bad faith and/or fraud.

The bill was also known as the "Melina bill," for Melina Tumpkin, the nine-year-old daughter of Conyers's Detroit office manager, who has been diagnosed with exposure to "toxic" mold. Tumpkin, her sister, and her mother were forced to flee their new home less than a month after moving in because Melina's asthma attacks worsened considerably. After several inspections by various private and local government agencies, *Stachybotrys* was found under the newly installed carpeting.

Finally, today there are many more news and magazine articles, books, television shows, and Web sites that deal with mold and mold-related problems. A comprehensive list follows in Chapter 9. For the latest news and information about mold-related issues, readers may also visit the author's Web site at www.moldauthor.com. To contact the author, e-mail: vicki@moldauthor.com.

Note: Home owners now have a new best friend in their war on mold: Dogs! Long used for sniffing out drugs, weapons, and missing people, dogs are now being trained in the U.S. to use their highly sensitive snouts to locate hidden mold inside homes, schools, and office and apartment buildings. Swedish dog-handlers were the first to develop the idea of using dogs to find hidden mold, according to Thomas Diederich, author of How to Find Hidden Microbial Growth With a Mold Dog, *a paper he presented at the Indoor Air Quality conference held in Sacramento, California, in 2001.*

MORE MOLD RESOURCES

airbrains.org
Why Are New Homes Moldier? by Arnold Mann
Web site: www.airbrains.org/Newhomemold.html

American Industrial Hygiene Foundation
The Facts About Mold: For Everyone
Web site: www.aiha.org/governmentaffairs-pr/html/
mold-consumer.htm

California Department of Health Services
Mold in My Home: What Do I Do?
Web site: www.cal-iaq.org/mold0107.htm

Canada Mortgage and Housing Corporation
Fighting Mold—The Homeowners' Guide
Web site: www.cmhc-schl.gc.ca/en/burema/gesein/
abhose/abhose_ce08.cfm

Centers for Disease Control and Prevention
Air Pollution and Respiratory Health/Mold
Web site: www.cdc.gov/nceh/airpollution/mold/

CBSnews.com (48 Hours)
An Insidious Mold
Web site: www.cbsnews.com/stories/2000/03/02/
48hours/main167069.shtml

Homeowners Against Deficient Dwellings
Web site: www.hadd.com

Indoor Air Quality Association
Mold Resources
Web site: www.iaqa.org/mold_resources.htm

Insurance Information Institute
Hot Topics and Insurance Issues/Mold
Web site: www.iii.org/media/hottopics/hot/mold/

insure.com
*Farmers Insurance must cough up $32 million
in Texas toxic mold verdict*
by Vicki Lankarge
Web site:
www.insure.com/states/tx/home/moldverdict601.html

Killer mold is nothing to sneeze at
by Vicki Lankarge
Web site: www.insure.com/home/mold.html

Mold-Help.org
Web site: www.mold-help.org

MoldRelief, Inc.
Web site: www.moldrelief.org

The Mold Source
Web site: www.themoldsource.com/

MoldUpdate.com
Web site: www.moldupdate.com

National Institute of Allergy and Infectious Diseases/National Institutes of Health
Mold Allergy
Web site:
www.niaid.nih.gov/publications/allergens/mold.htm

news-press.com
Mold is new threat in real estate world
by Frank D'Alessandro
Web site:
www.news-press.com/biz/today/020908frankcol.html

New York City Health Department
Facts About Mold
Web site:
www.ci.nyc.ny.us/html/doh/html/epi/epimold.html

Guidelines on Assessment and Remediation of Fungi in Indoor Environments

Web site:
www.ci.nyc.ny.us/html/doh/html/epi/moldrpt1.html

New York Times Magazine
Haunted by Mold by Lisa Belkin
Web site: www.nytimes.com

Policyholders of America
Web site: www.policyholdersofamerica.org

**Pulmonary Hemorrhage and Hemosiderosis
in Infants**
Web site: www.gcrc.meds.cwru.edu/stachy/default.htm

Realty Times
*Mold, A Mounting Concern for Homeowners,
Builders*
by Michele Dawson
Web site: www.realtytimes.com/rtnews/rtcpages/
20020108_mold.htm

**University of Minnesota/Environmental
and Health Safety**
Stachybotrys/Indoor Fungi Resources
Wed site: www.dehs.umn.edu/iaq/fungus/stachybotrys/

USA Today
Mold getting a costly hold on homes
by Rochelle Sharpe
Web site: www.usatoday.com/news/nation/2002/06/20/
mold-usat.htm

USAWeekend.com
Mold: A Health Alert
Web site: www.usaweekend.com/99_issues/991205/
991205mold.html

United States Environmental Protection Agency (EPA)
A Brief Guide to Mold, Moisture, and Your Home
Web site: www.epa.gov/iaq/molds/moldguide.html

An Office Building Occupant's Guide to Indoor Air Quality
www.epa.gov/iaq/pubs/occupgd.html

Biological Pollutants in Your Home
www.epa.gov/iaq/pubs/bio_1.html

Fact Sheet: Flood Cleanup—Avoiding Indoor Air Quality Problems
www.epa.gov/iaq/pubs/flood.html

Indoor Air/Asthma
www.epa.gov/iaq/asthma/links.html

Indoor Air—Mold/Moisture
www.epa.gov/iaq/pubs/moldresources.html

Indoor Air/Schools
www.epa/iaq/schools/links.html

Mold, Moisture, Mildew
www.epa.gov/iaq/molds

INDEX

ACKNOWLEDGMENTS

Because no author's work exists in a vacuum, I have many people to thank for helping me bring this book to completion.

First of all, thanks to Mary Glenn, my editor at McGraw-Hill, for finding me in the first place, and her assistant, Ed Chupak, for his attention to details great and small.

Thanks also go to my former colleagues at the *Daily Hampshire Gazette* in Northampton, Massachusetts, for giving me such a warm and wonderful place to begin my writing career. You'd be hard pressed to find any better writers and editors than Debra Scherban, Margot Cleary, Suzanne Wilson, and Jim Foudy.

Also, many thanks to my former colleagues at insure.com, particularly Amy Danise for recognizing a terrific story when she sees one, and Dan Nahorney for his insightful editing, journalistic passion, and friendship. I'm not sure I should thank him for dubbing me "Your Moldness."

Several organizations and governmental agencies were instrumental in my ability to produce this book. Special thanks and recognition goes to the California Department of Health Services, the Centers for Disease Control, the Insurance Council of Texas, the Insurance Information Institute, the Minnesota Department of Public Health, the National Association of Realtors, the

New York City Department of Health, the Policyholders of America, the Texas Department of Insurance, the Texas Office of Public Insurance Council, the University of Minnesota (Department of Environmental and Health Safety), and the United States Environmental Protection Agency.

I would also like to acknowledge the many people—contractors, homeowners, insurance media specialists, attorneys, realtors, researchers, and scientists—who took the time to return my phone calls and patiently answer my questions. Many thanks to Joseph Annotti, Melinda Ballard, Albert Betts, Robert Brand, Rod Bordelon, Jim Davis, Rick Gentry, Don Griffin, Robert Hartwig, Mark Hanna, Everette Lee Herndon, Jr., Bill Holder, Lee Jones, Greg Long, Russell Riggs, Jeanne Salvatore, Justin Schmitt, Phil Supple, Mike Trevino, and Karen Wilson.

I would be remiss if I failed to thank the many amazing professionals dedicated to improving this nation's health care industry that I had the pleasure of working with in my role of health insurance writer at insure.com. It was my interest in the potential adverse health effects of mold exposure that first prompted me to write about the subject. Many thanks to Peter Ashkenaz, Sue Blevins, Jacques Chambers, Jamie Court, Karen Donelan, Dr. Harvey Frey, Paul Fronstin, Larry Gelb, Joe Luchok, John Metz, Karen Pollitz, Dr. Deborah Peel, Dr. Linda Peeno, Dr. Chuck Phillips, Kathy Thomas, and Greg Scandlen.

Heartfelt thanks also go to my family and friends for their support while I regaled them with mold trivia and tidbits during this project. Thanks to David and Marilyn

Redding, Dennis and Betty Redding, Marie McIsaac, Rebecca Ververs, Richard and Michelle Varin, Lori Bellengreri, and the entire Lankarge clan, including my mother-in-law, who was under the impression that I was writing a book about "moles." Sorry Helen, I don't know how to stop them from eating your flower bulbs.

Finally, my gratitude to Debra Carney, a wonderful writer and my dear friend. Doo, thanks for being there on so many steps of this journey.

ABOUT THE AUTHOR

Award-winning reporter **Vicki Lankarge** is an accomplished journalist, business writer, editor, and nonfiction author with more than twenty years of experience covering consumer issues. She launched her writing career in 1985 as a reporter for the *Daily Hampshire Gazette* in Northampton, Massachusetts, where she wrote news and feature articles on topics including education, government, technology, small businesses, and health care. Her feature article on oncologist George Bowers, M.D., won first place in its category at the 1988 New England Associated Press News Executives Association Annual Awards. In 1990, Vicki left full-time journalism, launched her freelance writing career, working as a marketing consultant, and founded her own Web development company.

In 2000, Vicki joined insure.com, a consumer-oriented insurance news Web site. Her work at insure.com required her to understand and balance complex scientific, financial, regulatory, and political aspects of topics in the dynamic health care field. One of her articles on medical privacy was cited in testimony given by Dr. Deborah Peel before the Judiciary Committee of the United States House of Representatives' hearing on genetic privacy on September 12, 2002.

As Senior Editor, Vicki served as a lead spokesperson for insure.com in major media appearances. Through media joint ventures, her work appeared on such highly visible Web sites as America Online, CBS Marketwatch, and MSN.com. She lives with her husband and their two children in West Hartford, Connecticut, where she continues to write about health care, personal finance, and popular culture.